# In the tin

Sid is in the tin.

It is dim in the tin.

# Pam is at the tin.

Pam taps the tin.

The tin tips.

Sid tips.

# Sid is mad!

**In the tin**      **Level 1, Set 2: Story 8**

# Before reading

**Say the sounds:** s a t p i n m d
Ensure the children use pure sounds for the consonants without the added "uh" sounds, e.g. "mmmm" not "muh".

**Practise blending the sounds:** tin Sid dim Pam taps tips mad
**High-frequency words:** in it at    **Tricky words:** the is
**Vocabulary check:** dim – a dim light is dark, not bright; mad – angry or annoyed

**Story discussion:** What is Sid doing in the cover picture? Why do you think he's doing this?

**Teaching points:** Check that children can say the phonemes /s/ /a/ /t/ /p/ /i/ /n/ /m/ /d/, and that they can identify the grapheme that goes with each phoneme.
Check that children can recognise exclamation marks, and know how to read sentences with exclamation marks with appropriate expression.
Check that children can identify and read the tricky words: the, is.

# After reading

**Comprehension:**
- Who is this story about?
- Who tapped the tin?
- Why was Sid mad at the end?
- Do you think Pam meant to make Sid mad?

**Fluency:** Speed-read the words again from the inside front cover.